Letters to Heaven

CHRISTINA WILSON

Archway Publishing books may be ordered through booksellers or by contacting:

Archway Publishing
1663 Liberty Drive
Bloomington, IN 47403
www.archwaypublishing.com
1 (888) 242-5904

Because of the dynamic nature of the Internet, any web addresses or links contained in this book may have changed since publication and may no longer be valid. The views expressed in this work are solely those of the author and do not necessarily reflect the views of the publisher, and the publisher hereby disclaims any responsibility for them.

Any people depicted in stock imagery provided by Getty Images are models, and such images are being used for illustrative purposes only.
Certain stock imagery © Getty Images.

Interior Image Credit: Christina Wilson

ISBN: 978-1-4808-9225-5 (sc)
ISBN: 978-1-4808-9226-2 (e)

Print information available on the last page.

Archway Publishing rev. date: 07/01/2020

To my boys, Sammy and Jakie,
who are my heart.
In memory of our special times
writing letters to heaven.

It was a beautiful day. The sun was shining, and the birds were singing.

But Sammy and Jakie were feeling very sad.
Their daddy had died, and they
missed him very much.

Mommy said she had an idea about how to make them feel better.

Mommy got two balloons and some markers.

Mommy gave each boy a marker and a balloon. She said they should each write their daddy a letter on the balloon.

Sammy and Jakie wrote special messages to their daddy.

They also made beautiful pictures.

When they were done, Mommy
said, "Let's go outside."

They took their balloons out
to their backyard.

Then they held onto their balloons and climbed to the top of the play set.

Mommy told Sammy and Jakie they should let their balloons go, and their letters would fly to Daddy in heaven.

Sammy and Jakie let the balloons fly. They watched the balloons go higher and higher until they disappeared into heaven.

Then Sammy and Jakie began to smile. They felt very happy they got to send their daddy a letter.

Now, whenever Sammy and Jakie feel sad or miss their daddy, they send him letters to heaven.

In case you want to send your own letters to heaven, here are some helpful hints:

Use a solid-colored, helium-filled balloon.

Use felt-tip markers so the balloon does not pop while writing on it.

Make sure to release the balloon in an area free of trees or anything that the balloon can get stuck on or pop it.

Make sure there are not any utility, power, or electrical wires in the area where you release your balloon.

Author Biography

Christina Wilson wrote this children's book for her two sons, who were five and seven years old when their father died and who sent letters to their daddy just as the story describes. She currently lives in Boca Raton, Florida.

Printed in the United States
By Bookmasters